Retirement Planning for Law Enforcement Officers

How to Build

$1,000,000.00

Private Retirement Plan ™

Jim Clark

Published by

J. Charles Clark Publishing
a division of J. Charles Clark Consulting, Inc.
a member of the Clark Group of American Companies

ISBN 978-0-578-96207-8

Printed in the United States of America

Revised 2021

Special Dedication

This book is dedicated to Robert E. Houseworth, Sr., a Christian businessman who believed in a 20-year-old would-be entrepreneur enough to help him launch his career. Thank you for believing in me, Bob.

Foreword

I met Jim Clark and his Private Retirement Plan™ in 2001. While I had been practicing business law and estate planning for some time, I was relatively new to the then freshly burgeoning field of Retirement Planning for Middle America.

At the very outset, I was thoroughly impressed with the simplicity, power and effectiveness of Jim Clark's Private Retirement Plan™. For once, it appeared the tables would be turned **in favor** of the working man and woman. From that time to this day, I have used the Private Retirement Plan ™ for hundreds of my own clients as well as for myself.

In my nearly 30 years of legal practice, I have NEVER, and I mean NEVER, seen a system that is as right for clients as it is for the practitioner as is the Private Retirement Plan™ created by Jim Clark.

So, if you are a **working man or woman** and want to know why you're falling behind, this book, Retire Younger, Richer will tell you EXACTLY why as well as show you how to transform your situation.

If you are a **financial professional** and want to TRULY help your clients and stand head and shoulders above the competition, Retire Younger Richer will also show you how to do just that… and so much more.

Jim Clark is not only a truly brilliant man, my mentor, and colleague, he is also my friend. And it is with my highest recommendation I commend this book Retire Younger, Richer to anyone who wants to change their financial life. Read Retire Younger Richer, implement its directives, and just see what happens.

Kevin O. Pritchett, Esq.
Law Office of Kevin Pritchett, Inc.

Table of Contents

Prologue

If you have worked for 20 years, and you have earned at least $50,000 per year, you have earned $1,000,000.00 in your working lifetime. HOW MUCH CASH do you have now?

You take my point. It's difficult to save cash. WHY is it difficult to save cash? Because we pay everyone else first, before we pay ourselves. We pay the rent or mortgage, we pay the car payment, we pay the utilities, and on, and on, and on. By the time we think about putting some back for ourselves, there's nothing left to put back. And so it goes until one day we wake up and it's time to retire.

In my view, the Number One advantage we have in using the Private Retirement Plan™ to save for retirement is forced savings; it forces us to PAY OURSELVES FIRST. You simply build it into your budget, just like any other "bill". Then, when you look up one day and it's time to retire, you have the money to really enjoy retirement; you have the money to do the things you didn't have time to do while you were working. THAT is the position in which the wise man finds himself.

"There is treasure to be desired and oil in the dwelling of the wise; but a foolish man spendeth it up."

Proverbs 21:20

Do you need retirement planning?

Retirement Planning

Do you need retirement planning?

This could be the most important question of your financial life. I've been asking this question for a long time, and I can tell you that the response I get today is remarkably different than it used to be. People used to tell me they didn't need retirement planning, because they had a retirement plan at work, or a 401k plan, or Social Security. They said that they were already retired and that their retirement was all set. They felt like all they had to do was deposit their checks, sit back, and enjoy their retirement. For the most part, they were right, then. This is now.

Today, in post-Madoff America, people are telling me they don't trust corporate retirement plans anymore because after having worked for 30 or 40 years some Madoff might rob the company's retirement plan and run off with their money. And, they're saying that after saving for 30 or 40 years in their 401k plan, the stock market might crash again, and they'll be wiped out again; and, they're telling me that Social Security is a joke. NO ONE believes in Social Security anymore, because no one has confidence in the government's ability to handle money properly. What's the bottom line? Everyone knows that if they're going to have any money when they retire, they're going to have to do some personal retirement planning.

The Have Nots are staying HOME. They ain't going nowhere, and they ain't doing nothing, until the day they die.

The Haves and the Have Nots

There are two categories of retirees; there are the Haves and the Have Nots. The Haves are those who HAVE done personal retirement planning, and they have money saved outside of their company retirement plan or their 401k. The Have Nots are those who have NOT done personal retirement planning, and they do not have money saved outside of their company retirement plan or their 401k.

There's a BIG difference in how the Haves and Have Nots live during retirement. When the Haves get up in the morning, if they decide they would like to live in a different house, they call the realtor and look at houses because they CAN AFFORD to buy a new house. When the Haves get up in the morning, if they would like to drive a different car, they go to the dealership and look at new cars because they CAN AFFORD to buy a new car if they want one. When the Haves get up in the morning, if they would like to take a little trip, they call their travel agent or log on to Let'sGo.com because they CAN AFFORD to go on a little trip. You take my point? The Haves DO live differently during retirement because they have the money to do what they want to do; they have the money to do the things they didn't have time to do while they were working.

What about the Have Nots? Well, they have not. When the Have Nots get up in the morning they don't think about buying a new house because they CAN'T AFFORD to buy a new house; they just hope the roof on the house they have doesn't leak because they don't have the money to fix a leak in the roof. When the Have Nots get up in the morning they don't think about buying a new car; they just hope the car they have doesn't break down because they don't have the money to fix it.

The Have Nots have NOT, they're broke.

The Haves and the Have Nots

When the Have Nots get up in the morning they don't think about taking a little trip because they CAN'T AFFORD to take a little trip; they know the only trip they'll be taking is to the mailbox to see if the Social Security check is there, because it's been about a month since the last one arrived, and things are getting tight.

The Have Nots have NOT, they're broke. After 30 or 40 years of working day in and day out looking forward to retirement, they're flat broke. They're staying HOME. They ain't going nowhere, and they ain't doing nothing, until the day they die. Please pardon the slang.

Can you afford to gamble with your retirement savings? Can you afford to lose your retirement savings?

Three Financial Industries

When you think about it, there are only three places to which you can go to save or invest money for retirement; three "financial industries" if you will. The first is the stock industry (the stock market or mutual funds); the second is the banking industry; and, as odd as it might sound, the third is the life insurance industry. Three financial industries to which you can go to save or invest money for retirement; the stock industry, the banking industry, and the life insurance industry.

Stock Market

When it comes to saving for retirement, we can eliminate the stock market and mutual funds. Why? Because the money you invest in the stock market and mutual funds isn't guaranteed, and if it isn't guaranteed it isn't safe. Money invested in the stock market and mutual funds isn't guaranteed, and it isn't safe; so the stock market is NOT a place to save or invest for retirement.

When DOES a person invest in the stock market and mutual funds, and how much should he invest?

Invest in the stock market and mutual funds when you have money with which you want to gamble, and then you should invest only as much as you can afford to lose. Think of it this way, investing in the stock market and mutual funds is like buying a lottery ticket. You might win, and you might win big, but the odds are you won't, the odds are you'll lose.

Is there ANYONE who ever wins investing in the stock market and mutual funds?

Of course, there are the Big Boys of Finance. The Big Boys of Finance have the information to know when to get

Can you afford to gamble with your retirement savings?

in and when to get out, THEY are the ones who win investing in the stock market and mutual funds. They know when to get in and when to get out, and they have enough money to keep going when they lose. They CAN AFFORD to gamble, and they CAN AFFORD to lose from time to time. Can you? Can you afford to gamble with your retirement savings? Can you afford to lose your retirement savings? If you can't answer yes to both questions, stay away from the stock market and mutual funds when you save or invest for retirement. It really is just that simple.

Banks

When saving for retirement, we can eliminate the stock market and mutual funds, AND we can eliminate the bank. Why? Because the bank pays a POOR return.

Life Insurance Industry

There's no safety in the stock market and mutual funds, and there's no return at the bank. Where does a person go to save or invest for retirement? As odd as it might sound, the best place to save or invest for retirement is the life insurance industry. The life insurance industry? That's right. Today, the life insurance industry is THE industry to which millions of Americans are going to save for retirement. Times have changed in America, and times have changed in the life insurance industry. The life insurance industry has developed new products that are specifically designed for retirement; retirement policies and retirement annuities. The Private Retirement Plan™ is a nickname for just such a retirement policy; it's an incredibly powerful way to save for retirement.

SAFETY is the first reason to use the
Private Retirement Plan™
to save for retirement.

Four Great Reasons

There are four great reasons to establish your own Private Retirement Plan™. The Private Retirement Plan™ is safe, it pays an excellent return, the return grows tax-deferred, and, at retirement, it provides an income on which you pay no tax.

Safety

The most important thing with any retirement plan is safety. It just doesn't make sense to gamble with your retirement plan. Who wants to save for retirement for 30 or 40 years and then lose his money? Like Will Rogers said: "It's the return OF your money, not the return ON your money that counts."

Unlike the stock market, the life insurance industry is and always has been a safe place to save. Even during the Great Depression, when the stock market failed and the banking industry collapsed, only 13 life insurance companies were affected. Those 13 companies had $583 million of insurance in force, but at the time there was over $100 billion in force industry-wide. Not as much a 1% of all of the life insurance in force was affected by even the Great Depression. Less than one percent! The Private Retirement Plan™ is safe; you won't lose your money.

Return

The first return is the Guaranteed Minimum Lifetime Return, below which the rate will never go. Simply put, the Private Retirement Plan™ guarantees that for the rest of your life there will never be a day in which you don't earn at least something on your money. How does that compare with other places you can save or invest for retirement?

RETURN is the second reason to use the
Private Retirement Plan™
to save for retirement.

Ask yourself this question: if you put your retirement savings in the stock market or mutual funds, what return would the stock market or mutual funds guarantee for life? Correct, ZERO. There is NO guarantee on the money you put in the stock market, and there is NO Guaranteed Minimum Lifetime Return in the stock market or mutual funds. If you put your retirement savings in the stock market or mutual funds you might LOSE YOUR MONEY, and you might earn ZERO return

Now, ask yourself another question: if you put your retirement savings in the bank, what return would the bank guarantee for life? Correct again, ZERO. Even though the money you put in the bank is guaranteed, there is NO Guaranteed Minimum Lifetime Return. If you put your retirement savings in the bank, you might earn ZERO return.

The second return with the Private Retirement Plan™ is the Current Return. Unlike the Guaranteed Minimum Lifetime Return which stays the same for life, the Current Return can change. With the Private Retirement Plan™, you get BOTH returns. You get the Current Return which changes to give you a chance to keep up with the economy, and you get the Guaranteed Minimum Lifetime Return which guarantees that no matter what happens with the economy you'll earn at least something on your money. How does THAT compare with putting your retirement savings in the stock market, mutual funds, or bank?

Now, here's where the Private Retirement Plan™ gets exciting. YOU get to decide how the Current Return will be determined. You can choose to let the company from which you get your Private Retirement Plan™ decide what your Current Return will be, or you can have your Current return based on what the stock market does.

TAX DEFERRAL is the third reason to use
the Private Retirement Plan ™
to save for retirement.

"The stock market? I thought the whole idea of using the Private Retirement Plan™ to protect my retirement savings was safety". It is. If you choose to have your Current Return based on what the stock market does, the money you put in, and any growth you earn, is NOT in the stock market; it's in the Private Retirement Plan™. Only the RETURN you get is based on what the stock market does, not the money that you have. If the stock market goes up, the money that you have goes up; if the stock market goes down, the money that you have does NOT go down. What an exciting concept! You can participate in stock market growth if the market goes up, WITHOUT the risk of losing your money if the stock market goes down.

Tax Deferral

If you save for retirement in the stock market or mutual funds, you must pay taxes on any profits you earn immediately, in the year in which they are earned. If you save for retirement at the bank, you must pay taxes on any interest you might earn immediately, in the year in which it was earned. Not so with the Private Retirement Plan™. With the Private Retirement Plan™ you'll receive a statement from the company showing how much you earned, but you WON'T get a 1099. That's right. You'll get a statement showing how much you earned, but you won't get a 1099 because the Private Retirement Plan™ grows tax-deferred, which means you pay NO TAX until you actually take money out.

If you will have to pay taxes anyway, why not just pay them now? The key is the power of time and compound interest.

As long as the taxes are in your Private Retirement Plan™ YOU are earning a return on them until you take them out, so your Private Retirement Plan™ will grow faster.

NO-TAX RETIREMENT INCOME is the fourth reason
to use the Private Retirement Plan™
to save for retirement.

Put differently, tax deferral equals an interest-free loan from Uncle Sam, an interest-free loan on which YOU earn a return. As Judge Learned Hand said, considering the time use of money, a tax-deferred at least seven years is effectively avoided. Now I ask you, who are we to argue with Judge Learned Hand?

No-Tax Retirement Income

NO TAX INCOME AT RETIREMENT is the fourth reason to use the Private Retirement Plan™ to save for retirement. At retirement, there's a LEGAL way to receive an income on which you pay NO TAX. No tax? That's right. With the Private Retirement Plan™ your money is safe, it earns an excellent return, it grows tax-deferred, and at retirement you can receive an income on which you pay no tax.

You can start for almost any amount.

How Much Does It Take?

Does it take a lot of money to get started? No, it does not. As long as you meet the minimums for your age, you can start for almost any amount. Then, as time goes on and your circumstances change, you can increase the amount you put in, you can decrease the amount you put in, and you can add extra money at any time. YOU call the shots with the Private Retirement Plan™.

What if I die before I retire?

Before Retirement

What if something happens before retirement?

Death

What if I die before I retire; what would be done for my family?

First, the stock market and mutual funds: What would your family get if you died, and you were using the stock market and mutual funds to save for retirement? If you're using the stock market and mutual funds to save for retirement, and you died, all your family would get would be the amount you had invested, plus or minus some profit or losses, less any taxes that had to be paid. That's it. If you use the stock market or mutual funds to save for retirement and you die, all your family will get will be the amount you have invested, plus or minus some profit or losses, less any taxes that must be paid.

Second, the bank: What would your family get if you died, and you were using the bank to save for retirement? If you were using the bank to save for retirement, and you died, all your family would get would be the amount you had saved, plus a little interest, less any taxes that had to be paid. That's it. If you use the bank to save for retirement and you die, all your family will get will be the amount you have saved, plus a little interest, less any taxes that must be paid.

Third, the Private Retirement Plan™: What would your family get if you died, and you were using the Private Retirement Plan™ to save for retirement? Again, the Private Retirement Plan™ is a remarkably different and superior way to save for retirement than the stock market, mutual funds, or bank. In this example, I'm assuming you

What if I get disabled before I retire?

are a 25-year-old male who saved $300.00 per month for retirement (remember, you can start for more or less, and you can change the amount as time goes on). Since the Private Retirement Plan™ is a life insurance policy that's designed for accumulating money and tax-preferenced earnings, there's an IMMEDIATE death benefit for your family of $500,000.00.

You may have just started your Private Retirement Plan™, and you may have only put in $300.00, but even if you died on the first day that your plan is approved, there would still be an immediate death benefit of $500,000.00 for your family TAX FREE and PROBATE free. Section 101 of the Internal Revenue Code says the immediate death benefit is income tax free. Section 2052 says it's estate tax free (as long as you are under the limit), and the probate laws say it's probate free if the beneficiary designations are structured properly. Not one penny will be lost in taxes or probate. There is NO OTHER WAY to save for retirement wherein these benefits exist.

Disability

What if I get disabled before I retire?

Again, your family is protected. If you become totally and permanently disabled, the company with which you have your Private Retirement Plan™ will continue to pay the costs of the immediate death benefit for you. So, if you die while you're disabled, your family will still get the $500,000.00 immediate death benefit, tax free and probate free. Then, if you recover, you pick up where you left off, and do NOT reimburse the company for the costs paid for you while you were disabled.

What if I have an emergency before
I retire and need money?

What happens if you are using the stock market, mutual funds, or bank to save for retirement and you get disabled? Who does what to protect your family while you're off work? Correct, no one does anything.

Emergencies

What about emergencies? What if I have an emergency before I retire and need money?

If you're using the stock market, mutual funds, or bank to save for retirement, there may be tax penalties if you try to take money out before you are age 59 1/2. Not so with the Private Retirement Plan™. If you have an emergency and need to take money out of your Private Retirement Plan™ before age 59 1/2, you may do so and there will be NO TAX PENALTIES. You call the shots with the Private Retirement Plan™. By the way, a new fishing boat, cottage on the lake, or sports car "qualifies" as an emergency.

College Savings

What if I need money for something other than an emergency?

The Private Retirement Plan™ is a very powerful way to save for retirement; it's also a very powerful way to save for your children's college expenses. In fact, you can use your plan for both by simply adding extra money from time to time. If Little Johnny goes to school, you can make a tax-penalty-free withdrawal to help pay his expenses; however, if Little Johnny follows in the footsteps of his Aunt Bonnie and Uncle Clyde, you can simply skip the withdrawal and let the money continue to grow for your retirement.

YOU control the Private Retirement Plan™, not your employer and not the government.

Who's at the Helm?

Who's at the helm? Who controls the Private Retirement Plan™?

Control is another issue. Does it ever seem to you that you're losing control over your financial destiny, especially with your retirement savings? That will not be the case with the Private Retirement Plan™. YOU control the Private Retirement Plan™, not your employer and not the government. You own it, you control it, and you make all the decisions. Moreover, the Private Retirement Plan™ is portable; if you change jobs, you take your Private Retirement Plan™ with you.

If you're an employer there's good news for you too. You can establish a Private Retirement Plan™ for yourself, and you do NOT have to establish one for your employees unless you want to. If you want to do something for your employees, you can legally pick and choose for which employees you will establish a plan and how much you will pay for each. Let's face it, some employees work hard and do their best, while others couldn't care less. Why do the same thing for both groups? Why not favor the ones who really care about you and your business? With the Private Retirement Plan™, YOU have the flexibility and control to do what you want to do. After all, it's your company and your money.

...you won't care about the penalties because they will have vanished before you retire...

Penalties for Early Withdrawal

Are there penalties for early withdrawal, or are there costs involved? Of course, there are. There are costs for the insurance elements, and there are penalties (surrender charges) for cashing out too soon. However, if you use the Private Retirement Plan™ properly, for long-term retirement savings, you won't care about the penalties because they will have vanished before you retire, or they will have diminished to the point that you can draw an income without incurring a penalty. Moreover, unlike the penalties for early withdrawal attached to a Certificate of Deposit (CD) at the bank, once the surrender charges with the Private Retirement Plan™ vanish, they NEVER reappear.

Editor's Note: Every time a CD at the bank renews, the penalty period renews.

How much money will you have at retirement?

Retirement

You don't die, you don't get disabled, and you don't have to cash in early for an emergency, what about retirement

When can you retire?

You can retire at any age. Unlike a 401k Plan, pension plan, profit-sharing plan, or IRA, there are no age 59 ½ tax rules; you do NOT have to wait until you are age 59 ½ to retire. If you feel you have enough saved when you're 40, or 45, or 50, you can retire. You decide, not your employer, and not the IRS.

How much money will you have at retirement?

That's up to you, and the decisions you make. Three factors make all the difference:

First, WHERE you save for retirement is crucial. This example shows the difference between using the Private Retirement Plan™ and saving at the bank. The stock market and mutual funds have not been included because they aren't safe: be smart, don't gamble with your retirement.

Second, the AGE at which you begin is important. The younger you start, the more you'll have when you retire; so, start as soon as you can.

Third, the AMOUNT you put in makes a big difference. The more you put in, the more you'll have at retirement; so, put in as much as you can each month and put in extra money as often as you can.

What's the bottom line? Use the Private Retirement Plan™ to save for retirement, start as soon as you can, even if it's for a small amount, and put in as much as you can. You WILL retire younger, richer.

The Private Retirement Plan TM should be called
"The Best Kept Secret in Finance".

Private Retirement Plan ™ vs Bank

$300.00 / Month

	Bank	PRP
Total Put in to Age 65	$ 144,000	$ 144,000
Total Back at Age 65	**$ 221,796**	**$ 805,373**
Immediate Death Benefit	$ 300	$ 500,000

$600.00 / Month

	Bank	PRP
Total Put in to Age 65	$ 288,000	$ 288,000
Total Back at Age 65	**$ 443,592**	**$ 1,888,049**
Immediate Death Benefit	$ 600	$ 500,000

Comparison assumes current assumptions for the Private Retirement Plan™: and current interest rates for banks.

The question is, will you be a Have or a Have Not?

Epilogue

Well, that's about it. The Private Retirement Plan™ is safe, it pays an excellent return, the interest grows tax-deferred, and at retirement, it provides an income on which you pay no tax.

Now is the time to do a retirement review to decide whether the Private Retirement Plan™ is right for you. Time is slipping away. Before you know it, you'll be retired. The question is, will you be a Have or a Have Not?

Index

Public Notice

The author is not an attorney, nor does he give legal advice. The reader is advised to seek professional counsel with regard to his retirement planning, including, but not limited to, the concepts discussed herein. Neither the publisher nor the author accepts any liability for any consequences resulting from the reading of this book.

Private Retirement Plan™ is a nickname for an Equity Indexed Fixed Universal Life insurance policy. The Private Retirement Plan™ discussed herein is an imaginary plan offered by an imaginary company. It is offered only as the catalyst for the research of an actual plan.

Investments in the stock market referenced herein refer to common stock.

Taxable earnings referenced for the stock market, mutual funds, or bank are germane for earnings from non-qualified accounts.

Income and withdrawals on which you pay no tax achieved through policy loans; loans that you do NOT have to repay.

To avoid probate, a named beneficiary other than the owner's estate must be named.

The assumptions illustrated for the bank are based on current interest rates as of 03-17-16, no tax illustrated. The assumptions illustrated for the Private Retirement Plan ™ are based on the past performance of the stock market which may or may not be realized again. The lifetime minimum guaranteed return discussed for the Private Retirement Plan™ is set by the issuing company.

Jim Clark is an award-winning internationally-published author. He is the recipient of the International Poetry Society's coveted Editor's Choice Award for his outstanding book of romantic poems:

May I Dream?

A collection of poems on matters of the heart.

Jim Clark Books

Jim Clark books are exciting. There are four genres: Retirement Planning, Romance, Life on Earth, and Textbooks. Regardless of whether you're feeling romantic, planning your retirement, protecting your estate, or preparing for a new career, you'll find the right book in Jim Clark's outstanding collection.

Jim Clark books carry a three-fold purpose: to inform, to entertain, and to raise awareness that there are children in America who go to bed hungry. Profits from Jim Clark's books are donated to feeding hungry American children.

Jim Clark books are J. Charles Clark Publishing publications. This and other outstanding books by the author may be purchased at:

www.jimclarkbooks.com

To learn how you can help feed every hungry child in America visit

jimclarkamerican.com/children.

Made in the USA
Monee, IL
04 November 2026

67385488R10030